LEON MARCHAND

The Swimming Superstar

An inspiring biography for young readers

Terry J. Clark

LEON MARCHAND

LEON MARCHAND

TABLE OF CONTENT

INTRODUCTION

Have you ever dreamed of swimming faster than anyone else in the world? Imagine the thrill of diving into a pool, splashing through the water, and reaching the finish line in record time. That's what life is like for Leon Marchand, a real-life swimming superstar!

Leon didn't always know he would be a champion. Like many kids, he loved to splash around in the water when he was little. Growing up in France, Leon's days were filled with swimming in pools, having fun, and playing with his friends. But something was different about him. He wasn't just a good swimmer—he was fast! And not just fast, but determined to get even better.

His journey from being a playful swimmer to becoming one of the world's top athletes didn't happen overnight. It took years of hard work, early morning practices, and learning how to stay strong even when things got tough. Along the way, Leon broke world records, won medals, and represented his country on the biggest stages, including the Olympics!

But what makes Leon's story truly special is how he never gave up on his dreams. He inspires kids everywhere to believe in themselves, keep practicing, and always push for greatness—even when things feel impossible. In this book, you'll discover how Leon followed his passion, worked hard, and achieved his dreams. Who knows?

LEON MARCHAND

After reading his story, you'll be inspired to chase your own dreams—whether it's swimming or something else!

Let's dive in and discover the amazing journey of Leon Marchand, the swimming superstar!

CHAPTER 1: A SPLASHING START

Leon Marchand is a young swimmer from France who has become one of the fastest swimmers in the world! Born on May 17, 2002, Leon grew up loving water. His passion for swimming started when he was just a little boy, and he never stopped chasing his dream. What makes Leon's story even cooler is that his dad, Xavier Marchand, was also a swimmer who competed in the Olympics, just like Leon would one day do.

Leon is known for breaking records and winning medals in big competitions. He swims super fast in events like the butterfly, breaststroke, and medley races, where swimmers do different strokes in one race! Even though Leon is still young, he's already competed in the Olympics and made a name for himself on the world stage.

Leon's hard work, love for swimming, and determination make him a true champion, and he inspires kids all around the world to follow their dreams!

Growing Up with Water Dreams

Leon Marchand's love for water began when he was just a little boy. Imagine a toddler who couldn't wait to jump into the water! That was Leon. While some kids might feel scared or unsure near the pool, Leon felt right at home. Whether it was splashing in the shallow end, diving into the deep end, or simply playing games with his friends, the pool was his favorite place to be.

Growing up in the beautiful city of Toulouse, France, Leon was lucky to be around lots of water. He spent his summers at the pool, swimming as much as he could. He didn't just play—he practiced! While other kids played around, Leon would try to swim faster and farther each time. He loved the way the water felt as he glided through it. It was like he belonged in the water.

Leon wasn't always the fastest swimmer. Like any kid, he had to learn, and sometimes he even struggled. But Leon's excitement to improve never faded. He set small goals for himself, like learning how to dive better or swim underwater longer. Every time he reached a goal, it made him want to do more.

Leon's early love for swimming wasn't just about winning—it was about having fun, feeling free, and dreaming big. Little did he know that those childhood days of swimming for fun would one day turn him into a champion!

Family of Champions

Leon's passion for swimming wasn't just a coincidence. He grew up in a family that loved sports, especially swimming! His father, Xavier Marchand, was a famous swimmer too. Imagine growing up with a dad who knows all about racing, training, and winning medals. Xavier wasn't just any swimmer—he was an Olympic swimmer, representing France at the highest level.

Having a dad like that was both exciting and inspiring for Leon. From a young age, 'Leon would hear stories about his father's swimming adventures. Xavier would share tips, tricks, and advice about what it takes to be great in the pool. But what Leon loved most was how his dad never forced him to swim. Xavier wanted Leon to find his own love for the sport.

Leon's mom was also very supportive. Even though she wasn't a swimmer, she cheered Leon on from the sidelines, always making sure he had what he needed to succeed. Leon's family wasn't just about winning—they believed in having fun, working hard, and being the best you could be, no matter what.

LEON MARCHAND

With both of his parents encouraging him, Leon knew he had the support he needed to chase his dreams. But there was something special about following in his dad's footsteps. Seeing his father's medals and hearing about his Olympic experiences made Leon believe that he could achieve great things too.

Leon's family taught him that success isn't just about talent—it's about hard work, dedication, and, most importantly, loving what you do. And that's exactly what Leon did—he loved swimming, and he was ready to make a splash just like his dad!

CHAPTER 2: LEON'S 's FIRST SWIM MEET

The Race That Changed Everything

Leon Marchand had always loved swimming for fun, but nothing prepared him for the excitement of his first swim meet! He was still young, just a kid, when he entered his first real race. Imagine the feeling of standing on the pool deck, the smell of chlorine in the air, and the buzz of excitement all around. The other swimmers were stretching, coaches were shouting encouragement, and the crowd was cheering.

LEON MARCHAND

Leon felt both excited and nervous as he walked toward the starting block. He had practiced hard for this moment, but now it was real! His heart was racing as he stepped up, toes curled over the edge, waiting for the whistle. When the starting signal sounded, Leon dived into the water with all his strength. Splash! He kicked and pulled through the water, focusing on everything he had learned.

As he swam, Leon felt something different. The cheers from the crowd faded away, and it was just him and the water. Stroke by stroke, he pushed himself forward, faster and faster. When he touched the wall at the end of the race and lifted his head out of the water, something amazing happened. He had won!

Leon couldn't believe it—he had just won his first race! The excitement of his victory was like nothing he had ever felt before. His teammates and family cheered for him, and Leon realized this was the moment that changed everything. Winning that race gave Leon a taste of victory, and it made him want to experience that feeling again and again.

Discovering His Passion

After his first swim meet, something clicked for Leon. Swimming had always been fun, but now it was becoming something much bigger for him. That feeling of standing on the podium, getting a medal, and knowing all his hard work had paid off—it was unforgettable. Leon began to understand that swimming wasn't just a hobby or a fun way to spend time with his friends. It was something he was really good at, and more importantly, something he loved.

He began to look at swimming differently. Every practice became a chance to get better. Instead of just swimming for fun, he started setting goals for himself. Maybe he could swim faster or perfect his technique. Maybe one day, he could compete in bigger competitions, or even follow in his dad's footsteps and swim in the Olympics. Leon realized that if he put in the hard work, he could achieve anything he set his mind to.

Leon's coaches noticed this change in him too. He started showing up earlier to practices and worked even harder than before. While other kids might have gotten tired or given up, Leon just kept pushing himself. It was during these times that Leon discovered his true passion for the sport. He loved the feeling of swimming fast, the challenge of competition, and the thrill of racing.

From that moment on, Leon was no longer just swimming for fun—he was swimming because it was his passion, something he wanted to get serious about. He dreamed of becoming the best swimmer he could be, and with every lap, he was one step closer to making that dream a reality.

CHAPTER 3: TRAINING LIKE A CHAMPION

Early Morning Practices

Being a great swimmer doesn't happen by accident. It takes hard work, and for Leon Marchand, that meant waking up before the sun! Imagine getting out of bed while it's still dark outside, and instead of snuggling under the covers, you're heading to the pool. That's what Leon did almost every day. Even though it wasn't always easy, Leon knew that early morning practices were important if he wanted to be the best.

Leon would wake up early, grab his swim bag, and head to the pool while most kids were still asleep. The water would be cool and calm as he dived in to start his training. Some mornings were harder than others—he'd be tired from school or maybe not in the mood to swim. But Leon had a goal, and he was determined to work for it. Every stroke, every lap, and every practice brought him closer to becoming the swimmer he dreamed of being.

During these early practices, Leon worked on everything from his technique to his endurance. He practiced swimming faster and perfecting his turns. Even though the practices were tough, Leon knew that each one helped him improve. It wasn't always fun to wake up early, but Leon had a passion for swimming, and he was willing to put in the hard work.

Leon's dedication showed that being a champion doesn't just happen in races—it happens in the quiet moments when no one else is watching, like those early mornings in the pool when Leon was giving it his all.

Pushing Beyond Limits

Training like a champion isn't just about showing up; it's about pushing yourself to get better, even when it's tough. For Leon, some days were really challenging. The practices became harder as he advanced, and his coach expected more from him. Some days, his muscles were sore, and he felt exhausted. He had to swim more laps, do harder drills, and even practice after school when he was tired from the day.

But instead of giving up, Leon learned to push through these tough moments. He reminded himself that every challenge was helping him grow stronger and faster. When the practices felt impossible, Leon focused on his goals—becoming the best swimmer he could be and racing against the best in the world.

One of Leon's biggest challenges was learning how to balance everything—school, friends, and swimming. Sometimes, he felt like there weren't enough hours in the day. But Leon had something special: a never-give-up attitude. Even on the toughest days, he kept going. He knew that champions weren't just the people who won races; they were the ones who kept trying, even when things got hard.

There were moments when Leon didn't win or didn't swim as fast as he hoped, but instead of feeling defeated, he used those experiences to get better. He learned from every race and every practice. Pushing beyond his limits helped Leon realize that anything is possible if you believe in yourself and never give up.

By working hard and always pushing forward, Leon showed that the road to success might be tough, but it's also filled with exciting possibilities for those who keep trying.

CHAPTER 4: MAKING WAVES IN FRANCE

Winning His First Medals

After all the early mornings and tough practices, Leon Marchand finally had his moment to shine. His hard work was about to pay off when he entered a big competition in France. This wasn't just any race—it was a chance for Leon to show how much he had improved. As he stood on the pool deck, heart pounding with excitement, Leon knew that this race could be the moment he had been waiting for.

When the starting whistle blew, Leon dived into the water with everything he had. He swam faster than ever before, giving his best effort in every stroke. As he touched the wall at the end of the race and looked up at the scoreboard, Leon couldn't believe his eyes. He had won his first medal!

The shiny, gold medal placed around his neck was more than just an award—it was a symbol of all the hard work he had put in over the years. The crowd cheered, and Leon's family and friends beamed with pride. This was his first taste of success, and it felt amazing.

But winning the medal wasn't just about being the fastest. For Leon, it was proof that hard work and dedication could make his dreams come true. That medal made him want to keep going, to keep swimming faster and aiming higher. Leon's victory wasn't just a win in the pool—it was the beginning of something much bigger.

Becoming a National Star

As Leon continued to swim in more competitions, something incredible happened: his name started to become well-known all across France! His victories piled up, and he was winning medals in local and national competitions. Leon wasn't just another swimmer anymore—he was a rising star. People began to notice how fast he was, and his story of hard work and determination inspired young swimmers everywhere.

Leon's performances in national competitions showed that he had something special. He was not only winning races, but he was also breaking records! Swimmers, coaches, and fans across the country began talking about Leon, wondering how far this young swimmer could go. His success even got him noticed by France's national swim team coaches, who saw Leon as a future champion who could compete on the world stage.

Even though Leon was becoming famous, he stayed humble and focused on getting better. He never let the attention or the medals distract him from his love for swimming. In fact, the more he won, the more he wanted to improve. Leon knew that there was always something to work on, whether it was perfecting his strokes or getting stronger.

Leon's story also became a source of inspiration for kids who dreamed of being swimmers. Many young swimmers in France began to look up to Leon as a role model. His journey showed them that with hard work, dedication, and a never-give-up attitude, they too could achieve great things.

Leon Marchand wasn't just winning races—he was making waves all across France, becoming a symbol of what it means to follow your dreams and never stop believing in yourself.

CHAPTER 5: WORLD RECORDS AND BIG DREAMS

Breaking Barriers

As Leon Marchand continued to grow as a swimmer, his hard work began to pay off in a huge way. He wasn't just winning medals—he was breaking records! Imagine swimming so fast that you set a new world record, becoming one of the fastest swimmers ever. That's exactly what Leon did, and it took everyone by surprise, even his toughest competitors.

LEON MARCHAND

Breaking a record isn't easy. It takes months, even years, of training, discipline, and staying focused. Leon knew this, and he wasn't afraid of putting in the work. Every time he jumped into the pool, he gave it his all, pushing himself to swim faster and better. He practiced harder, did more drills, and listened carefully to his coaches. Leon didn't just want to win races—he wanted to be the best in the world.

The day Leon broke his first world record was unforgettable. He was competing in a big international meet, swimming against some of the fastest athletes on the planet. As the race started, Leon used every ounce of energy he had, racing through the water with powerful strokes. When he finished and looked at the scoreboard, the crowd erupted in cheers. He had not only won the race but had also set a new world record!

Leon's accomplishment was more than just a personal victory. It was a sign that he had reached a level few swimmers ever reach. He was no longer just a national star—he was one of the fastest swimmers in the world. But Leon knew that breaking records wasn't the end of his journey. It was just the beginning.

Setting New Goals

Even though Leon had already achieved so much, he didn't stop there. Instead of resting after his big wins, Leon decided to set new goals. He knew that the best athletes never stop improving, and there was always something more he could achieve. Whether it was breaking another record, mastering a new swimming technique, or preparing for the next big competition, Leon's mind was always focused on what was next.

One of Leon's biggest dreams was to compete in the Olympics and represent France on the world stage. The thought of swimming against the best athletes in the world excited him. But even before the Olympics, there were plenty of other goals to chase. Leon wanted to swim faster, become stronger, and continue breaking records.

Leon also began to think about how he could inspire other kids to set their own goals. He knew that success wasn't just about winning races—it was about believing in yourself and working hard to reach your dreams. Leon hoped that by sharing his story, other young swimmers would be motivated to push themselves and set big goals, just like he had done.

No matter how many records Leon broke or medals he won, he never lost sight of the most important thing: the love he had for swimming. Every time he got into the pool, he remembered why he started in the first place. Swimming was his passion, and it was the driving force behind all of his success.

For Leon, the journey was just as exciting as the victories. He knew that with each new goal he set, there was another challenge waiting for him. And with every challenge, there was a chance to grow, improve, and chase even bigger dreams. Leon's story shows that no matter how much

LEON MARCHAND

you achieve, there's always room to dream bigger and reach higher.

CHAPTER 6: COMPETING ON THE WORLD STAGE

Facing the Best Swimmers

Leon Marchand had worked hard to become one of the fastest swimmers in France, but now it was time to take on the world! Competing in international competitions meant racing against the best swimmers from every country. Imagine stepping up to the pool, knowing that the person next to you is one of the fastest swimmers on the planet. That's what Leon faced every time he competed internationally.

LEON MARCHAND

At first, the idea of competing against such strong swimmers might have seemed a little scary, but Leon was ready. He had trained for years to reach this level, and he knew that he belonged there. As he traveled to different countries for big swim meets, Leon's excitement grew. It was a chance to test himself against the world's best, and he welcomed the challenge.

Each competition was tougher than the last. The swimmers were faster, the races were closer, and the pressure was higher. But Leon didn't let that stop him. He knew that the only way to get better was to compete against the best. With every race, Leon learned something new—whether it was about his technique, his speed, or how to stay focused under pressure.

Leon's first international wins were special. Standing on the podium, hearing the cheers from fans all over the world, and seeing the French flag raised in his honor—it was a moment he would never forget. Competing on the world stage wasn't just about medals for Leon—it was about proving to himself that he could rise to any challenge.

The Olympic Dream

For many athletes, competing in the Olympics is the ultimate dream, and for Leon Marchand, it was no different. Ever since he was a kid, Leon had imagined what it would be like to swim at the Olympics, representing France on the biggest stage in the world. Now, after years of hard work, that dream was coming true.

36

LEON MARCHAND

Getting ready for the Olympics was no easy task. The training became even more intense, with early mornings, long practices, and extra time spent working on every detail of his technique. Leon knew that at the Olympics, every second mattered. Even a tiny mistake could make the difference between winning a medal or missing out. So, he practiced over and over again, making sure he was as prepared as possible.

As the day of the Olympics approached, Leon felt both excited and nervous. He had dreamed about this moment for so long, and now it was finally here. When he arrived at the Olympic Village, surrounded by athletes from all over the world, the excitement was electric. It was incredible to be part of such a huge event, knowing that millions of people would be watching.

When it was time for his race, Leon took a deep breath and reminded himself why he was there. He had trained for this moment, and now it was his time to shine. As he stepped up to the starting block and looked out at the Olympic pool, he felt a surge of energy. This was the race he had been waiting for his entire life.

Swimming in the Olympics wasn't just about competing for a medal—it was about fulfilling a lifelong dream. And for Leon, being part of the Olympics was one of the greatest achievements of his life. Whether he won or not, the journey to the Olympics taught him the value of hard work, dedication, and believing in yourself, no matter how big your dreams are.

CHAPTER 7: INSPIRING THE NEXT GENERATION

Leon's Message to Young Swimmers

Leon Marchand knows what it feels like to have a big dream, just like many young swimmers around the world. He started as a kid who loved splashing around in the pool, but through hard work and dedication, he became one of the fastest swimmers in the world. Now, Leon has a message for kids who love swimming and have dreams of their own: "If I can do it, so can you!"

LEON MARCHAND

Leon wants young swimmers to know that swimming is not just about winning races or earning medals. It's about enjoying the journey and having fun in the water. He remembers when he was a kid, how much he loved being in the pool, racing his friends, and feeling the excitement of every stroke. Leon believes that if you love what you do, the hard work becomes easier, and the victories will follow.

Leon also understands that swimming can be tough sometimes. There will be early mornings, hard practices, and moments when you feel like giving up. That's why his message to young swimmers is simple: "Keep going"! Every lap you swim, every race you enter, and every challenge you face brings you closer to your dream. Whether you want to swim in the Olympics or just be the best swimmer you can be, the most important thing is to never lose sight of why you started.

Leon encourages young swimmers to always believe in themselves. Even when things get hard or when you feel like you're not improving, remember that every champion started as a beginner. Just like Leon did, you can achieve anything if you work hard and stay dedicated to your dream.

Never Giving Up on Your Dreams

Leon's journey to becoming a world-class swimmer wasn't always easy. There were days when he faced challenges that seemed impossible to overcome. But Leon never gave up, and he wants to share that important lesson with kids everywhere: "Never give up on your dreams".

When Leon first started competing, he wasn't always the fastest swimmer in the pool. He faced tough races, and there were times when he didn't win. But instead of feeling discouraged, Leon used those moments to learn and improve. He knew that every challenge was an opportunity to get better. Even when things didn't go his way, he stayed focused on his goals.

Leon wants kids to know that chasing your dreams isn't always a straight path. Sometimes there will be obstacles or setbacks, but that doesn't mean you should stop. In fact, those challenges are what make the journey so special. Leon believes that "the hardest moments can be the most important ones" because they teach you

42

how to be strong, keep going, and never lose hope.

For Leon, perseverance was key. He didn't become a champion overnight—it took years of dedication, practice, and a positive attitude. He learned that the most important thing was to love what he was doing and to believe in himself, no matter what. Leon's story shows that even when things seem tough, if you keep pushing forward, you can achieve amazing things.

Leon hopes that his story inspires kids to dream big and work hard. Whether your dream is to be a swimmer, a doctor, an artist, or anything else, the key is to never give up. Leon's message is clear: "You can achieve your dreams if you keep believing, keep working, and keep swimming toward success"!

21 fun facts about Leon Marchand

1. Born to Swim: Leon Marchand comes from a family of swimmers—his father, Xavier Marchand, was an Olympic swimmer for France!

2. Olympic Dream: Leon made his Olympic debut at the 2020 Tokyo Olympics, competing in the 400-meter individual medley.

3. Hometown Hero: Leon was born in Toulouse, France, a city known for its love of sports.

4. Young Champion: By the time he was 18, Leon had already won several national championships in France.

5. World Record Breaker: In 2023, Leon broke the world record in the 400-meter individual medley, becoming one of the fastest swimmers in history.

6. Loves IM Events: Leon's favorite swimming events are the individual medley races, where swimmers compete in four different strokes—freestyle, backstroke, breaststroke, and butterfly.

7. Training in the USA: Leon trains at Arizona State University under coach Bob Bowman, who also coached swimming legend Michael Phelps!

8. Dual Athlete: Before fully committing to swimming, Leon also played water polo.

9. Nickname: His teammates sometimes call him "The Machine" because of his incredible endurance and power in the pool.

10. Multilingual: Leon is fluent in both French and English.

11. Big Fan of Michael Phelps: Leon grew up idolizing Michael Phelps and now trains under Phelps' former coach!

12. Record Holder in France: He holds several French national records in various swimming events, including the 200-meter and 400-meter individual medleys.

13. Loves to Surf: When Leon isn't training, he enjoys surfing and spending time at the beach.

14. Family Legacy: His dad competed in the 1996 and 2000 Olympics, so Leon was always inspired by his father's achievements.

15. Nutrition Focused: Leon pays close attention to his diet, making sure to fuel his body with the right foods for peak performance.

16. Loves Music: Before big races, Leon likes to listen to music to help him stay calm and focused.

17. Animal Lover: Leon loves animals, especially dogs, and has a pet dog at home in France.

18. University Studies: In addition to swimming, Leon is also a student at Arizona State University, studying computer science.

19. Fun Personality: Despite being super focused in the pool, Leon is known for his playful and fun personality with his teammates.

20. Youngest French Star: Leon became the youngest French swimmer to win a world championship title in 2022!

21. Big Goals: Even after breaking world records, Leon is still focused on achieving even more—including winning gold at the Paris 2024 Olympics!

CONCLUSION

Leon Marchand's story is one of dedication, hard work, and passion. From a young boy who loved splashing around in the pool to becoming a world record-breaking swimmer, Leon has shown that with determination, anything is possible. His journey reminds us that dreams can come true if you believe in yourself and work hard every day.

Leon wasn't born a champion. Like many kids, he started by simply loving the water. He spent hours practicing and improving, even when it was tough. He faced challenges along the way, but instead of giving up, Leon pushed through, knowing that every hard moment would lead him closer to his dreams. He wasn't just racing against others—he was racing against his own limits, always trying to be better than he was before.

What makes Leon's story so special is that he didn't just focus on winning medals—he also wanted to inspire others. Leon understands that being a great swimmer is not just about being fast, but also about staying positive, never giving up, and enjoying the journey. He hopes that young swimmers everywhere will learn from his story and chase their own dreams, just like he did.

Whether Leon is breaking records, winning medals, or setting new goals, he is always thinking about the future and how he can continue to grow. His message to young readers is simple: never stop dreaming, keep working hard, and believe in yourself. Just like Leon Marchand, you too can become a superstar in whatever you set your mind to!

Leon's journey isn't over yet. With the Olympics and many more races ahead, his story will continue to inspire generations of young athletes. So, the next time you dive into a pool, remember Leon's story and keep swimming toward your own dreams!

Questions

Answer the following Questions:

1. What inspired Leon Marchand to start swimming?

_____

2. Who in Leon's family was also a swimmer and helped inspire him?

_____

3. What was the name of Leon's first big swimming competition?

_____

4. How did Leon prepare for his swim meets?

_____

5. What is Leon's favorite swimming event?

_____

6. Which world record did Leon break?

7. What country does Leon represent when he competes internationally?

8. Where does Leon train now, and who is his coach?

9. What does Leon want to inspire young swimmers to do?

10. What big event did Leon dream of competing in from a young age?

_____

Puzzles

Solve the following puzzles:

Word Scramble:

Unscramble the letters to find out what type of race Leon loves most.

- IDNVEULIA MDYEEL

Unscramble the letters to reveal Leon's motto:

- D A R E T O D R E A M

Crossword Clue:

Leon broke a world _____.

True or False:

LEON MARCHAND

Leon started swimming because he loved being in the water from a young age. True or False

Fill in the Blank:

Leon's father, Xavier Marchand, was also an Olympic _____.

(a.) Swimmer (b.) Footballer (c.) hockey player

Matching:

Match the event to the number of strokes in the race.

- a) 100m Freestyle = 4 strokes)
- b) 200m Individual Medley = 1 stroke

Find the Word:

In the word grid below, find the word "**Champion**."

C H A M P

I B G F I

Z E L S O

T C D H N

Q N A R A

Multiple Choice: What sport did Leon play before focusing only on swimming?

- a) Basketball
- b) Water Polo
- c) Soccer

Made in the USA
Las Vegas, NV
10 December 2024

13825713R00036